Strength in Verse: Poetic Triumphs Over Fibromyalgia

Bethan Howells

BookLeaf Publishing
India | USA | UK

Strength in Verse: Poetic Triumphs Over Fibromyalgia © 2023 Bethan Howells

All rights reserved.

No part of this publication may be reproduced, stored in a retrieval system, or transmitted, in any form or by any means, electronic, mechanical, photocopying, recording or otherwise, without the prior written permission of the presenters.

Bethan Howells asserts the moral right to be identified as author of this work.

Presentation by *BookLeaf Publishing*

Web: www.bookleafpub.com

E-mail: info@bookleafpub.com

ISBN: 9789358317053

First edition 2023

I dedicate this collection to all those currently facing their own battles, whether it's the relentless struggle of a chronic illness or other challenges life presents. Know that you are not alone in your journey, and within these pages, may you discover comfort, fortitude, and the reassurance that your strength serves as an inspiration to others.

ACKNOWLEDGEMENT

I would like to thank all the many wonderful people I have met on my journey so far, who have inspired me to keep going every day and find healing ways to deal with whatever life throws my way. From the many doctors and practitioners to my very dearest friends and family, this collection is born from your caring words and calming touches.

PREFACE

I am not a poet. In fact, growing up I had a rather reluctant relationship with poetry and it was my older sister who slowly opened my eyes to the beauty and power of reading and writing poems. I distinctly remember that when she first encouraged me to use poetry as an outlet for anxious thoughts, I was somewhat sceptical and wrote a poem entitled "I can't write poetry" in an attempt at witty rebellion. Later that same night, I pondered on how secretly enjoyable I had found the experience and set about putting into verse some of my experiences of living with a chronic illness. Some years later, expressing my feelings through poetry feels as natural and necessary as breathing.

For a long time, I kept my poems private. However, when I slowly gained the courage to share them with my closest friends and family, many remarked on how the poems helped them truly appreciate and understand my experience of living with fibromyalgia. As it is an invisible and often misunderstood illness, it struck me that poetry could provide an invaluable window into the reality of living with this chronic condition that brings with it pain, anxiety, fatigue and insomnia, along with many other symptoms. Everyone's journey facing a chronic illness is unique and, whilst these words encapsulate only my own experience, it is my hope they resonate with others facing similar fights and inspire them to give a voice to their personal experiences as well as raising awareness and understanding of some of the realities of living with fibromyalgia.

What am I?

Thought stealer,
Pain provider,
Strength eroder,
Ache maker,
Overwhelm giver,
Energy drainer,
Worry messenger,
Insomnia player,
Concentration catcher,
Tingling taunter,

I am fibromyalgia.

A four-letter word

There is a four-letter word
That controls my life
Every decision
Every day

It strikes like a dagger
When I least expect
Leaving scars
On my heart

A four-letter word
It can't fully convey
The depths
of the feelings

It has me in its grasp
Its mesmerising spell
No, this four-letter word
It's not love, it's pain

Constant Pain

Every day we can be sure of,
The setting of the sun.
The falling and rising tide,
Love or heartache for someone.

There's another thing I'm sure of,
When I wake up every day.
The other thing I know for sure,
Is that I will be in pain.

The Pain Monster

You scream all day long
Angry, harsh, relentless
Taunting, Shouting
Look at me!
If I try to ignore you
You just shout louder
Stomping around like you own the place
Will you never rest?

Describe your pain

I know it's difficult
Sharp?
Dull?
Throb?
Ache?
All of them? Really?
What about on a scale 1 to 10?
A 7?
That's high
10 is the worst pain possible
Like labour or being stabbed
Do you want to change your answer?
A 5?
That's better.

Just One Moment

What I wouldn't give
To live for just one moment
To swing my arms with carelessness
Without feeling that tenseness

What I wouldn't give
To live for just one moment
To sink back and relax in a chair
Without any aching there

What I wouldn't give
To live for just one moment
To dance under the pouring rain
Without a single pain

Are you sitting comfortably?

Are you sitting comfortably?
Once a phrase that brought anticipation
At the story soon to be told
Never really considered
Comfort was a given, the story the excitement

Are you sitting comfortably?
Now a constant nagging question
With the answer always no
Are you the least uncomfortable?
Would be more appropriate

PAIN

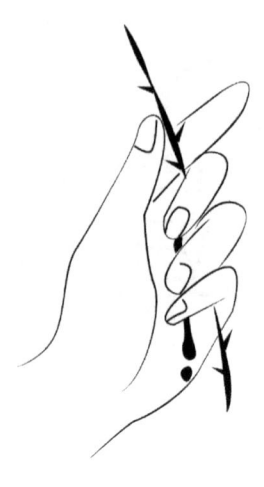

Perpetual Agony Increasing Notably
Pangs And Instant Nausea
Probing Arrows Inside Neck
Physical Anguish Ignited Needlessly
Pouncing And Intruding Nightly
Persistent Ache Is Never-ending
Powerful And Insidious Nemesis

Life without pain?

Without night-time, the sun wouldn't seem so bright
Without cold days, fire wouldn't be so welcomed
Without sadness, happiness wouldn't feel so joyful
Without heartbreak, we wouldn't love so strong
Then maybe, just maybe
Without pain, I wouldn't be so grateful

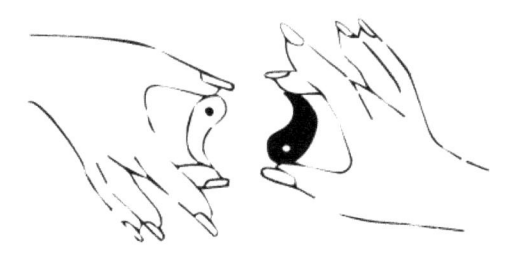

Insomnia

The no man's land between wake and sleep
Too tired to do
But too awake to dream
Whirring Whirring
Thoughts Feelings
Toss Turn
Get up Get down
When will this nightmare end!
Can a nightmare end if you're not asleep?

Excruciating Tiredness

Eyes Stinging
Muscles Tensing
Bones Aching
Head Pounding
I'm tired I say
Me too they say back
But you don't understand
I am really really tired

The Anxiety Bubble

I have a bubble
In my tummy it lies
And when I feel anxious
It grows in size

A bubble of unease
It floats through my day
Invisible to others
As I wish it away

The more I wish it
The bigger it grows
Until it fills me
From my head to my toes

Oh, how I wish
That bubble would pop
But whatever I do
I can't make it stop

Then I remember
And take a breath deep
And away the bubble
Begins to creep

In that moment
I can keep it at bay
But I know that bubble
Is here to stay

Panic Attack

Chest tightening
WILL
Breathing faster
THIS
Head spinning
EVER
Heart thudding
END
Breathe, breathe

A Foggy Day

When you're in the middle of a sentence,
And forget what you wanted to say,
It's a foggy day.

When you walk the supermarket aisles,
But don't know what you came for,
It's a foggy day.

When the word is on the tip of your tongue,
And you just can't place it,
It's a foggy day.

When you pull up at the services,
Because you've forgotten where you were heading,
It's a foggy day.

When you watch a whole TV show,
And can't remember what happened,
It's a foggy day.

When you have a million things to do,
But don't know what they are,
It's a foggy day.

But the fog will clear
And reveal a bright blue sky
Sometimes you just have to
Sit and wait out the storm

In the Brain Fog

My thoughts wander
Lonely as a cloud
Yet somehow together
All at once

Fitting and flying
One to another
Never managing to rest on one
Not long enough

The grey mist looms
Settling wherever it can hold
Consuming every nook and cranny
It's in control now

What I Want

I want to come to work today
I want to do my job
I want to be a success you know
I want to do it all

I want to make you dinner today
I want to wash up too
I want to help you out you know
I want to do it all

I want to go out with you today
I want to get all dressed up
I want to have good fun you know
I want to do it all

I want to do it all
But sometimes my body says no
And what I want most of all
Is not to lose it all

(so I can no longer say) I am a failure

I am a failure
So I can no longer say
I keep going
Although I try my best
It is hard
I can't do this
So it would be wrong to say
I am resilient
I know
I am useless
And I refuse to believe
I am good enough

Now reread from the bottom to the top.

An open letter to fibromyalgia

Dear fibro,
Old friend, always by my side
I have to tell you how I feel
I can no longer hide

Dear fibro,
Old chum, there's something I must say
I know you've had the upper hand
But it's time I had my way

Dear fibro,
Old pal, you never let me rest
Always nagging, prodding, moaning
It puts me to the test

Dear fibro,
Old mate, you are too intense for me
I try my best to accept you
But for once please let me be

Dear fibro,
Old friend, always by my side
I have to tell you how I feel
So in peace we can reside

Giving Thanks

I'm thankful to my body for keeping me breathing
And thankful to my brain for still believing
I'm thankful to my heart for holding on to hope
And thankful to my friends for helping me cope
I'm thankful to the sun for rising each day
And thankful to my parents for showing me the way
I'm thankful for being able to write this refrain
And thankful for the strength to manage the pain

The Long Road We Travel

It's a long road we travel.
Sapping energy all the time.
And sometimes it can feel,
Like a never-ending climb.

But when the road feels too long,
Just take small steps ahead.
With one foot in front of the other,
You can keep a steady tread.

A heavy load to carry,
Up the hillside so steep.
Share it with a friend,
So you don't fall in a heap.

When the path gets steeper still,
And you feel like you could drop.
Take a break, a breather,
Just whatever you do, don't stop.

You'll finally reach that mountain top,
And revel in pure delight.
Even though around the corner,
There's another hill in sight.

Each hill you'll conquer the same way,
Taking it in your stride.
And every time you reach a peak,
Allow time to enjoy the pride.

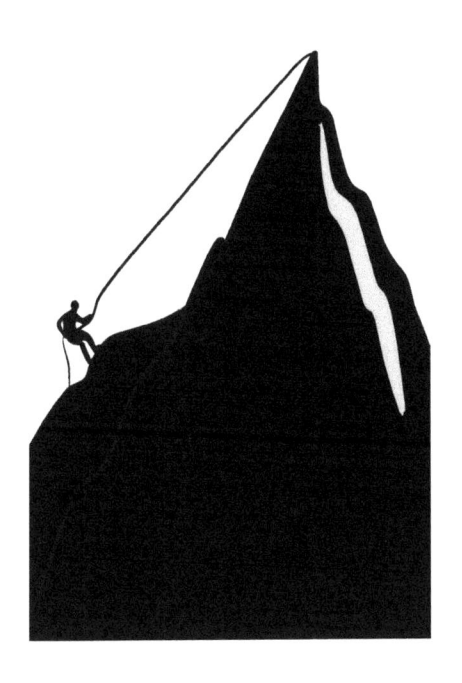

The Fibro Butterfly

Such a simple thing,
The gentle flutter,
Of a butterfly wing,
Can unfold a whirlwind.

Such a fragile thing,
A butterfly wing,
Vulnerable and delicate,
Bearing the weight of pain.

Yet a persisting thing,
That butterfly wing,
Dancing through the days
And darkest nights.

And a beautiful thing,
A butterfly wing,
Bringing with it hope,
Of a new spring.

Such a simple thing,
The gentle flutter,
Of a butterfly wing,
Can alter the path of life.

Milton Keynes UK
Ingram Content Group UK Ltd.
UKHW021032200524
442968UK00016B/1160

9 789358 317053